1   Introduction

Shamanism is the oldest religion on the planet!

In terms of human existence, it predates current day organized religions by tens of thousands of years. European cave paintings and carvings showing shaman date from the Paleolithic era. Graves of shamans 12,000-year-old and older have been discovered in Israel and the Czech Republic.

Shamans have played an essential role in the defence of the psychic integrity of their community for thousands of years.

They are pre-eminently the antidemonic champions; they combat not only demons and disease, but also black magicians... In a general way, it can be said that shamanism defends life, health, fertility [and] the world of 'light,' against death, diseases, sterility, disaster and the world of 'darkness'... What is fundamental and universal is the shamans struggle against what we could call the 'powers of evil. Shamans are not only able to foresee the future, but also to change the outcome. As an example, shamans can find out where food or game is located for the community, or avert threats to the community. This is a vital difference between shamanism and clairvoyance.[1]

We will look more in depth at Shamans, Shamanism and the mystical journeys they undertake to heal and help people with compassion and care.

This is the second book in the series on Shamanism and is complimentary to my books on Reiki. There is a direct link between the Shaman's Helping Spirits and Reiki Guides that help Reiki practitioners bring healing and comfort to people worldwide.

The Reiki, Shamanism, and essential loving mysticism are complementary to our YouTube video series, "Reiki With Candice, Mark, and Opame," and The Shaman Podcast on iTunes, Spotify, Google Podcasts, and more. Together, these expand on Reiki and what it means to be a shaman and enjoy the capabilities of a shaman.

Visit and subscribe to all of these as well as our blog, thepracticalshaman.ca.

Enjoy.
Mark Ashford, MSc,
Usui Tibetan Reiki Master and Teacher
www.markaashford.com
information@markaashford.com

---

[1] https://www.energy-shifter.com/shamanism-and-spiritual-techniques.html, "Shamanism, and Soul Retrieval - Spiritual House Cleansing."

2 Table of contents

3 Role of the Shaman

3.1 Healer and Guide

T he shaman is a healer. This is their principal role in the tribe and the community.

They have access to, and influence in, the world of benevolent and malevolent spirits, who typically enter into a trance state during a ritual, and practices divination and healing.

Soul journeying to understand what and why a person was ill and journeying to spirits that will help return health to the physical person is their primary and most essential role.

Mongol shamanism had ninety-nine deities:

- Fifty-five of these deities were White, i.e., Beneficents for mankind.

- Forty-four were Black, i.e., Terrible to all the evildoers of mankind and to the enemies of the Mongol Nation.

In total, they are the national gods of Mongol Shamanism. No commoner of any Mongol clan dared embarrass them with his insubstantial bagatelles, since they were the Spirits of Ancestors of every clan, the souls of dead chieftains, shamans, and shamanesses who during their life had devoted themselves to satisfying the requirements of the members of clans and who in the World of Spirits should solve the difficulties in the life of the members of their clans, commoners, and nobles and even serfs. [2]

Minor spirits of a clan's ancestors were divided into several classes. The largest among them was the class of the souls of the clans' chieftains, introduced after their death by a special solemn shamanist right to the communion of Clan Ancestors and thus becoming members of the communion and of the Benevolent Lord-Spirits who played a very important role in the life of a clan and its members.

Black shamanism is a kind of shamanism practised in Mongolia and Siberia. It is specifically opposed to yellow shamanism, which incorporates rituals and traditions from Buddhism. Black Shamans are usually perceived as working with evil spirits, while white Shamans with spirits of the upper world.

Other Souls and Spirits included…

- Souls of the Great Shamans: Protector-Spirits of the Clan

- Souls of the Simple Shamans: Guardian-Spirits of Localities

- The Three Spirits Accepting Supplication

---

[2] Yönsiyebü Rinchen, "White, Black and Yellow Shamans among the Mongols," *Ultimate Reality and Meaning* 4, no. 2 (1981).

Division of the gods and spirits of Mongol shamanism:

- White and Black deities

- Lord-Spirits of the clan

- Protector-Spirits of the clan

- Guardian-Spirits of the clan

- White Spirits of Nobles of the clan

- Black Spirits of Commoners of the clan

- Evil Spirits

Chinggis Khan, or Genghis Khan, the renowned Mongolian leader, practised Black Shamanism, though he himself was not a shaman.

The banner at the head of the Mongol Armies that subjugated China and got as far as eastern Europe was black. But this should not be confused with Chinggis Khan and his practice of Black Shamanism. A tribe would have black and white banners in the centre of their camp.

The banners were each guarded together with white and black Lord Spirits of the Clan. Nobles of the clan would escort the banners during ceremonies and feasts.

In battle, the black banner was believed to bring victory over Mongol enemies, while the white banner remained in camp.

3.2   Oracle

Shaman were astrologers and Oracles. Everyone, especially tribal leaders, wants to know what the future will bring. Will it bring war, will they be successful in the struggle? Will crops and animal husbandry be successful? Will the tribe merge with another through marriage?

The history of the shaman in this role goes back into the very remote past, before the advent of Buddhism in Tibet in the 7th century.

Historically, these Oracles, divination, and Astrology were a feature of Bon in pre-Buddhist Tibet. The Bon cosmology was divided into three worlds.

- The upper world of the gods.

- An intermediate world of spirits, of subtle beings.

- The solid or physical world we know as the earth.

Bon also held the spirit or soul of the individual, which was a world or realm of energy which humans are able to contact. For example, humans are able to connect with physical things, such as food, a chair, and other people. On the spiritual level, they are able to connect at the psychic level with other spirits and those on the different levels, such as the first and second.

When Buddhists brought Buddhist Dharma to Tibet, they were able to include the Bon world view on their own because Buddhism holds the view. The Buddhist world exists in three parts: one solid, one psychic and one mental.

The change happened when the famous tantric master Guru Padmasambhava came to Tibet and tamed the subtle world – the deities of the Bonpos - and bound them under oath to obey and defend the Buddhist teaching. He made these powers, which we can call deities, protectors of the Buddhist faith and of Buddhist practitioners. They became Cho sung, protectors of the Dharma. According to Tibetan tradition, he tamed these beings through the powerful invocation of mantras and powerful spells, which bound them to obey those who held the power of these spells. Guru Padmasambhava tamed these beings. He made them protectors of the Dharma and obliged or convinced them to help practitioners of Buddha Dharma by communicating, giving advice, foretelling the future and even healing people.[3]

The deities are sentient beings. They are beings, just like people or animals and anyone else, but without a body. They also have a mind or spirit, and a voice. Without a body, they cannot communicate with those who communicate on a bodily level. So, they are samsaric beings.

Samsara is the term for the everlasting cycle of being. It is the cycle of becoming and passing away, or the cycle of rebirths in the Indian religions of Hinduism, Buddhism and Jainism.

As such, they are not higher gods, as we would understand the great gods of India or Tibet. They are gods linked to the land, mountains, lakes and to the geographical features. We could in a way say that mountains and lakes are their bodily aspect. So, they are the subtle aspect: the speech and mind aspect of mountains, valleys, rivers, and lakes, especially mountains and lakes.

3.3   Continuity

They were the spiritual leader of a group or tribe. The belief and practice of Shamanism incorporate a range of beliefs, customs, ceremonies, and rituals regarding communication with the spiritual world in which their religious leader, the Shaman, enters supernatural realms, particularly when the tribe is facing adversity or needs to obtain solutions to problems afflicting the community, including sickness.[4]

They provided continuity to the tribe and a reliable connection to the spirit world. In this way, they were a communicator from the human physical world to the spirit world and back again.

They were an educator of people about the spirit world as well as about medicines and herbs and natural healing solutions. They kept the tribal stories, myths, and essential tribal wisdom that made the tribe they belonged to different from another.

---

[3] Dr Fabian Sanders, "Tibetan Oracles and Himalayan Shamans."
[4] warpaths2peacepipes.com, "Shaman."

They understood and passed down understanding of trance states, how to induce them and how to control them. Their clothing, symbolic regalia and objects were passed down to enrich subsequent generations of shamans.

They are the keepers of tradition, ancient texts, books, and scripts as well as the way things should be done. Songs, dances, music, and observance are also carried forward from shaman to shaman within the tribe.

Shamans usually have expert knowledge of medicinal plants native to their area, and an herbal treatment is often prescribed. It is believed shamans learn directly from the plants, harnessing their effects and healing properties, after obtaining permission from the indwelling or patron spirits.[5]

The chieftains and nobles may change, but the shaman remains.

3.4   Protector

One of a shaman's main functions is to protect individuals from hostile supernatural influences.

The shaman may act as psychopomp conducting the spirits of individuals who have just died to the proper refuge for dead spirits.

Psychopomp literally means "guide of souls") are creatures, spirits, angels, or deities in many religions whose responsibility is to escort newly deceased souls from Earth to the afterlife. They do not judge the deceased, but simply guide them. Appearing frequently on funerary art, psychopomps have been depicted at different times and in different cultures as anthropomorphic entities, horses, deer, dogs, whip-poor-wills, ravens, crows, vultures, owls, sparrows and cuckoos. When seen as birds, they are often seen in huge masses, waiting outside the home of the dying.[6]

---

[5] Wikipedia, "Shamanism."
[6] "Psychopomp."

4   Bon, Shamanism, and the Five Elements

Yungdrung Bon is the pre-Buddhist spiritual tradition of Tibet, and, when Buddhism was introduced into Tibet, it became part of the Buddhist religion, which makes it the original Buddhist religion of Tibetan people. It originated from the region known as Zhang Zhung, a kingdom west and north of Tibet.

The first Bon scriptures were translated from the language of Zhang-zhung into Tibetan. The works contained in the Bonpo canon we know today are written in Tibetan, but a number of them, especially the older ones, retain the titles and at times whole passages in the language of Zhang-zhung.

Yungdrung Bon was taught by Buddha Tonpa Sherab in Wol-mo Loong-Ring (Shambala). The Buddha's history can be traced back to over 18,000 years ago.

Beginning in the 8th century, Dharma, an Indian religion, also appeared. Since then, Tibet has had two major religious traditions; Yungdrung Bon and Dharma. Yungdrung Bon has five sub-schools and Dharma with five sub-schools under their umbrella, respectively. Both the traditions emphasize the generating of indiscriminate love and compassion and have similar views on the path. However, there are historical and geographical differences, etc.

Yungdrung Bon's teachings are based on the principle of indiscriminate love and compassion towards all and is the path of Theg-pa Chen-po or Mahayana in its approach. Many of the teachings are similar to those found in the five principal schools of Buddhism, especially the Nyingma-pa school, and are aimed at enabling all to access Enlightenment and freedom from the shackles of Samsara.

Many teachings in the Yungdrung Bon tradition are also similar to those in other major Tibetan spiritual traditions - everything from elaborate visualizations of tantric deities to the simplicity and immediacy of the Dzogchen meditations. They contribute to the richness and depth of the Bon heritage and its shamanistic practices, which carry a deep respect for nature and the spirits that abide in it and all around us.

A space may be considered sacred when we experience it close and intimate to ourselves. A shaman, seeing a mountain, the experiences the strength of the earth element represented by the tall powerful sight, which evokes a sense of devotion. The earth under our feet and the mountain is where things grow, where beings live. There is a raw, grounded force in the spirit of the earth mother and this is respected as a higher entity, a source of healing.

The shaman is an intermediary to the sacred, master of intuited knowledge, a sage and a master of scholarly knowledge, connecting above and below, inside, and outside, energy and matter.

The shamanistic and animistic belief system is strongly connected to nature and surrounding landscapes inhabited by gods and spirits to whom sacrifices are offered. The cosmos is divided into three worlds – the upper, the middle and the lower world, with the upper and lower worlds having seven more levels. The latter are inhabited by a hierarchy of gods and spirits, but deities are present in the middle world, the world of human beings. The shaman is the mediator between these three worlds, the realm of the spirits and the human world, capable of acquiring information from other spheres, reconciling gods and thereby healing. He is also able to control energies and fight with spirits and go through unthinkable physical transformations undergoing a symbolic death and rebirth during a shamanic ritual. He is the doctor, psychologist and priest and one of the most important figures in society.[7]

To a shaman, earth, water, fire, air, and space are all sacred. These five elements make up all things. When we think of the five elements, think beyond the simple label. Think of everything that is that elemental state. Air is everything that is a gas; water is everything that is a liquid; it also represents thoughts and communication. Earth is everything that is solid; it represents the physical body. Fire is everything that is a fire, or on fire, or fiery, and is our vital energy. Space is everything that is a void or nothingness, regardless of whether it is the space over our head in the night sky or the space between atoms at the atomic level. Space also represents higher spiritual realms.

Fire is important because it provides the energy for transformation from one state of matter to another. Fire heats water, from a solid, ice, into a liquid, water. If fire is allowed to continue, it transforms the liquid water into stream or a gas, which is now the element of air. Without fire, steam becomes a liquid again and if it is cold, a solid. Fire is worshipped in many yogic and Tantric rituals because it is the means by which we can purify, empower, and control the other states of matter.

Some elements naturally combine: earth and water, fire and air, for example. Others will eliminate each other, fire and water, for example. Water will put out fire, and fire will evaporate [turn to air] water, so, they need to be separated.[8]

Each element is responsible for different structures in the body. Earth forms solid structures, such as bones, flesh, skin, tissues, and hair. Water forms saliva, urine, semen, blood, and sweat. Fire forms hunger, thirst, and sleep. Air is responsible for all movement, including expansion, contraction, and suppression. Space forms physical attraction and repulsion, as well as fear.[9]

Modern society, however, has lost its connection to these elements; they hold little meaning. Land has become a vessel item; it is something to be bought and sold. When we build on land, there is no consideration for the spirits that exist in the earth, or the water that is diverted from its natural follow.

In Ayurveda, a Traditional Medicine from India, the same five elements appear and illness is defined as a deficiency or block in physical, emotional, and spiritual harmony that may leave an opening for disease. All objects and the human body are combinations of the five elements or the Panchamahabhutas: Akash (ether i.e., space), Vayu (air), Agni (fire), Jala (water), and Prithvi (earth).[10]

When we look down at the ground under your feet, all we see is tarmac or concrete; there is no connection to the natural earth. A shaman feels and interacts with the spirits of nature in a very complete and spirit focused way, which is astonishing and powerful.

---

[7] HELEN SAARNIIT, "The Khanty of Western Siberia- Elements of Shamanism as a Form of Cultural Identity."
[8] DR. SWAMI SHANKARDEV SARASWATI, "Purifying the Five Elements of Our Being - Yoga Journal.Pdf>," *Yoga Journal*.
[9] Ibid.
[10] A. H. Lichtenstein, A. Berger, and M. J. Cheng, "Definitions of Healing and Healing Interventions across Different Cultures," *Ann Palliat Med* 6, no. 3 (2017).

Bon Tantra, Dzogchen and shamanism offer widely divergent approaches, yet they are mutually supportive. They share at least one common essence: the elements of earth, water, fire, air and space are considered sacred; they are the underlying force of existence. Because they are sacred, all that arises from them, everything is also sacred.

Sacred means any situation where you encounter something that makes the experience of yourself the deepest and closest. Shamans see the earth as sacred earth, water as sacred water, fire as sacred fire, air as sacred air, space as sacred space. Modem society has almost entirely lost this meaning in nature. Land is seen only as a place to buy and sell and to build on. When you are in the streets of a city, nearly every single inch is solid cement and pavement—there's almost no connection with nature.

The shaman relates with the elements of nature in a gross, dualistic, very spirit-oriented way, but still in a way that is amazing and powerful.

In Tantra, through the visualization of syllables and symbols, channels and chakras, the five elements are experienced in the human body in the form of divine energy. Every part of our body is seen as a palace of the divine. When you see that way, feel that way, relate that way, you have a sacred dimension of experience.

In Dzogchen, it is the same but at the level of the mind. The Dzogchen practitioner works with all the elements like light. At the subtlest level, the elements are light, and luminosity, they are inseparable and united in their emptiness, the basis of everything. In Dzogchen, the elements are associated with the five wisdom qualities, or pure presences. For example, water is coupled with blue light and with mirror-like wisdom. The space element is associated with white light and with the wisdom of emptiness.

If the elements are balanced externally, then one will be physically healthy. From a tantric perspective, when elements are balanced, internally one feels joy, one feels love, one feels compassion, one feels balance or equilibrium. In Dzogchen, balance of the elements brings a unique experience of space and light. Grounding, flexibility, openness, and creativity these are qualities of the primordial energy of existence. Each connects differently, one at the raw level, one at the energetic level, and one at a purer level of mind and light.

Imbalance: In the physical, raw level, a person with an abundance of the earth element may be fat, or overweight. Energetically, they are lazy, dull, or depressed. They forget things and are slow suffering limited progress in personal or spiritual development. From the Dzogchen perspective, things are subtler: a lack of stability in meditation, of awareness of their connection to the base, concentration, and comprehension of sunyata. Yet, in the physical world, there is little if anything that is wrong; it is all internal.

At the beginning of our life, there is a balance of elements; you could say we are balanced. The world changes that.

Each of us has experiences that have a significant effect on who we are. There are other experiences which have less of an impact or maybe no impact at all. The experience is not as important as the meaning we extract from it. The meaning stays with us; collectively, all of them create who we are.

What is the story we tell ourselves about that experience? That's what affects who we are, future decisions we make, and how we interact with others.

For instance, my parents were divorced when I was 8 years old. The way that affected me is different than the way it affected other people who were in a similar situation. I remember noticing this as a teenager. I saw other kids with divorced parents and how they experienced it differently. It was even different between my siblings and me.

The meaning we create from our experiences, shapes and moulds us and creates who we are.

As we go out to face the world, we have so many good experiences and bad experiences, disappointments and hurts. We have so many intense experiences, but we don't necessarily have a way of processing them. As a result, these experiences can damage some of these elemental qualities. Maybe you have stability and then something tragic or traumatic happens; from there on, you just don't feel very well grounded any more.
If we have a very strong experience and are able to process it, it won't do anything to us. Being able to process means that you can feel it anyway, but it will not damage you. It will not change you. It will not weaken you. It will not make you lose some qualities. Being able to process means that it will energize you. You are clear with it. In some sense, it can make you grow, make you expand your consciousness and make you become wiser and more understanding.

Not being able to manage what is happening to us will certainly shake us. It is a question of degree. If you are quite a strong person and you are hit by that experience, it will take your strength away. Maybe you were happy; when you face it, it will take your happiness away. Somehow it will damage that particular quality.

The five negative emotions of anger, desire, ignorance, jealousy, and pride are related with the elements, too. Anger is related with air. Desire is related to fire, and so on. When one is more balanced, one can have more experience of love. When one is unbalanced because of too much air and a lack of earth or grounding, one can have an experience of anger instead. Anger feels like an explosion outward, like air blowing things away - we lose control. This is opposite the experience of when we get depressed, because of too much earth and not enough air.

Tantra literally means, loom, weave, or system. It refers to the traditions of Hinduism and Buddhism that co-developed most likely about the middle of the 1st millennium AD. The term Tantra, in the Indian tradition, also means any systematic broadly applicable "text, theory, system, method, instrument, technique or practice.[11]

In tantric visualization of syllables and symbols, channels, and chakras, the five elements are experienced in the human body in the form of divine energy. Our body is seen as divine. If we are divine, we have a sacred dimension to our experience.

Dzogchen[12] is at the level of the mind, light or pure thought. Because Dzogchen is all about light and thought, all the elements are considered to be light. Think of the luminosity of water; it is blue. In Dzogchen, water is luminous blue light; this is a mirror-like wisdom. In this way, the five elements the shaman is interacting with in nature are seen as unique qualities of wisdom or pure presence. The space element is white light and the wisdom or presence of emptiness.

―――――――――――――――――

[11] Wikipedia, "Tantra."
[12] "Dzogchen."

Each of the five elements is associated with different human experiences, emotions, temperaments, colours, illnesses, thinking styles, and so on. Each of the experiences invokes differing interactions of the five elements. If the elements are balanced externally, you could be thought of as physically healthy.

In tantric perception, when the five elements achieve balance, inside yourself you feel joy, love, compassion, or equilibrium and you experience these spontaneously.

In Dzogchen, balanced elements allow you to experience the different qualities of space and light. You are grounded, flexible, open, and creative all are experienced as delicate facets of the elemental energy of existence.

Tantric and Dzogchen devotees experience the five elements differently from each other and the shaman is different again. Rather like different languages, each may not understand the other when they describe the five elements. Yet all understand when inner heat is required to develop and experience the inner bliss of fire. A shaman connects at a raw level, the tantric follower connects at an energetic level, and the Dzogchen follower connects at a pure level of mind and light.

Imbalance of the elements manifests clearly in the physical dimension. A person with too much earth element may be overweight. They feel lazy, dull, or depressed. People with too much earth forget things, are slow, and have very little progression in their personal or spiritual development.

Imbalance from the Dzogchen perspective is very subtle. There is a lack of stability in meditation and awareness of their connection to the base is limited; they do not concentrate; they lack understanding of sunyata[13]. The person may be unbalanced, but they may also be unaware of it because there's nothing particularly wrong physically or psychologically.

Confusion in day-to-day life and a lack of stability is a deficiency of the earth element. A lack of creativity is a lack of the fire element. A lack of openness, a feeling of being shut down is a lack of space. A lack of flexibility is insufficient air.

Too much of any one element causes problems; too little of one element also causes problems. When you see the kinds of conditions and qualities that are manifesting, you can look within yourself and understand the causes on a deeper, emotional level.

At the beginning of our existence, there is a balance in the five elements. As we grow and experience life, as we experience good and bad events, disappointments, hurt, and success, we have to learn how to deal with them. We often struggle, and if one type of event or experience is repetitive, what was strong becomes weakened and unbalanced and the elements in us are damaged?

Ability to manage and deal with a traumatic event does not damage the elements in you. You are not changed by it. You are not weakened, but if the event is a happy one, you are also not overly strengthened. The event becomes a source of energy you can draw for future experiences. You are learning how to grow and evolve; you are more aware and your consciousness expands; you are wiser and more understanding.

_____

[13] "Sunyata."

If you have problems dealing with the situation, it will shake you; you become doubtful and uncertain. You lose confidence and strength; your inner core is reduced. Typically, a traumatic event saps energy and ability.

The five negative emotions are anger, desire, ignorance, jealousy, and pride. They are related to the five elements anger to air, desire to fire, and so on. If there is an imbalance of too much air, the person is considered to have too little grounding, that is, too little earth and that means anger instead of love when they are balanced. Anger expresses itself as an explosion outward from the soul, air blows things away and, by its nature, there is no control over things. An opposite example would be too much earth; it manifests as depression because there is insufficient energetic air.

If any element is impure or out of balance with another, disease and suffering may occur. Yoga helps us purify these elements and restore balance and health, and to unfold the inner powers and abilities contained in each element. In fact, yoga is one of the most powerful ways to restore health because it gives us the means to bring even those elements that are natural enemies into harmonious relationships with each other.[14]

As we retrieve the elements we heal, the sensation of healing may not be obvious, but wait, there will be a shift in you; you will start to become balanced and heal. Changes in the way you relate or behave changes. For example, if you have too little earth element, you are ungrounded and feel as if you are in chaos. After you retrieve the earth element, you feel so different and grounded.

To retrieve the elements, you need either a shamanic approach, a tantric approach or a Dzogchen approach, all express themselves differently.

The shaman understands the energy of the earth, drawing the quality of the earth element from the earth goddess, the earth spirit, or by connecting more with the raw earth. There are a lot of forms of shamanic practices. It's the same with tantric: There are meditation, contemplation and specific exercises to try to control the dominating qualities of the air, fire, and other elements. Dzogchen practices involve simply abiding, or being, while merging oneself with the subtlest qualities of the elements.

Yogic practices are also a convenient way to heal. Knowledge of the five elements is an essential prerequisite for more advanced yoga practice because the elements from the world we live in and the structure of our body mind. All yoga practices work on the five elements, whether we know it or not. Knowledge of the elements (tattwas) is also the basis of yoga therapy and of Ayurveda, traditional Indian medicine. Through consciously working with the elements, we learn how to attain and maintain health and also how to consciously enjoy a long and fulfilling life based on higher awareness. [15]

Death. Death represents the dissolution of the elements in a person. In death, earth melts into water, water into fire, fire into air, and air into space. In order to achieve liberation in the Bardo,[16] the intermediate, transitional, or liminal state between death and rebirth, one aims to experience one's self during the entire dyeing process. Maintaining clear presence in the subtler forms of elements and in the very subtlest element form of light, and even in the clear light of space.

---

[14] SARASWATI, "Purifying the Five Elements of Our Being - Yoga Journal.Pdf>."
[15] Ibid.
[16] Wikipedia, "Bardo."

In the past century, Western medicine has made extraordinary leaps through scientific methods in defining, diagnosing, treating, and, in many cases, curing diseases. However, its emphasis has been predominantly on disease and on organ focused specialties, and much less person centred. In contrast to other healing traditions, patients are extracted from familiar environments and moved into hospitals, often limiting interactions with the larger community. Psychosocial spiritual assessment is not routinely incorporated as part of a person's treatment plan, especially among the adult population.[17]

One must be cautious not to utilize complementary therapies as a tool isolated from the core philosophies of healing from where they originate. Western medicine has yet to tap deeply into the mind-body-spirit connection central to many other healing practices across cultures. In the coming decades, we hope for growing awareness and understanding about spirituality's impact on healing and wellness. This will likely be incorporated gradually into various aspects and levels of Western medicine's lexicon of diagnosis and healing techniques.[18]

The five colours of the five elements appear everywhere. Traditionally, prayer flags come in sets of five: one in each of five colours. The colours are arranged from left to right in a specific order: blue, white, red, green, and yellow. The five colours represent the five elements and the Five Pure Lights. Different elements are associated with different colours for specific traditions, purposes, and sadhana.[19]

Colour	Symbolizes	Negative emotions	Properties
Blue	Sky and Space	Ignorance	Accommodates all other elements
White	Air and Wind	Anger	Motion
Red	Fire	Desire	Temperature
Green	Water	Jealousy	Cohesion
Yellow	Earth	Pride	Solidity

---

[17] Lichtenstein, Berger, and Cheng, "Definitions of Healing and Healing Interventions across Different Cultures."
[18] Ibid.
[19] Wikipedia, "Prayer Flag."

5 Observance and Rituals

First, we need to change the way we think about the five elements. The five elements are in all things, and all things are sacred, but in modern society the connection to the sacred this view point has been lost for most people. Look at a car, for example, it contains all five elements. The earth provided the metal, water represents the liquids, gas, oil, and coolant; fire is combustible, air allows gasoline to burn, and space allows the car to exist. Stop thinking of it as "car" and instead see it as the interplay of the five elements. The five elements represent the five senses, the five fields of sensual experience, the five negative emotions, and the five wisdom. This is how to think about the elements.

In the Tibetan shamanic view, the five elements of earth, water, fire, air, and space are accessed through the raw powers of nature and through non-physical beings associated with the natural world. In the Tibetan tantric view, the elements are recognized as five kinds of energy in the body and are balanced with a program of yogic movements, breathing exercises, and visualizations. In the Dzogchen teachings, the elements are understood to be the radiance of being and are accessed through pure awareness.

Previously, we said the five elements and everything that arose from them are sacred. If we do not have a clear relationship to these sacred elements, we do not have a clear spiritual path. The observance and rituals the shaman performs on our behalf, when we are sick, or we do for ourselves if we know how, have become things that make us feel good, like a walk on a summer's day, or a nice meal.

As we consider our relationship to the sacred elements, be aware of the reinforcement repeating certain actions has in our own spirit. The person who always responds with anger, to people, things, pets, and the world in general is reinforcing and "stoking the fire" of negativity within themselves. Social groups and work environments that favour aggressive and fiery behaviour exaggerate these qualities and help suppress or diminish the other elements. However, someone who responds creatively to situations is also connecting to the fire element, but in this case the outcome is positive.

Imbalance of elements can be either lifelong or short term. Public speaking can be stressful. A person who has good balance and appears happy and relaxed but becomes anxious and stressed at the prospect of their public duties. Another person may become self-confident after drinking alcohol but otherwise be quiet and unobtrusive.

As elemental beings, we are in a relationship with everything and everyone around us. Hopefully, our relationships are supportive and enjoyable and help us grow and fulfil us. If those relationships are lacking, or of poor quality, that part of our existence is dying, buried, or hasn't been opened up to us.

5.1 Five Elements and Shamanism

Bon and Buddhism support four immeasurable qualities in ourselves that help support our spiritual path; they are love, joy, compassion, and equanimity. These are in us and can be brought into our awareness when we do or see something that supports these qualities, for example siting in the early morning sun, listening to music, being with people we love and care about. All qualities can be expressed through our approach to life and others; they also help us understand ourselves and our spiritual path.

To progress, we need to work with the elements and understand them. A powerful part of shamanistic practice is the knowledge and understanding that the elements contain numerous living, divine, goddesses, and powerful semi-divine beings. The shaman teaches us to value our inner self and externally, all of nature around us. In this progress, we need to understand that the shaman is unconcerned with philosophy he or she understands what is needed and what to connect to, what to manipulate and what to defend against to resolve the need.

The beauty of this practice and your spiritual path is that they are not static or simply a series of rituals performed repetitiously without thought or caring. This is an active practice that evolves and grows with your study, investigation, experimentation and understanding of what is best for your path and how you are progressing.

Bon teachings feature Nine Vehicles, which are pathway-teaching categories with distinct characteristics, views, practices, and results. Medicine, astrology, and divination are in the lower vehicles; then sutra and Tantra, with Dzogchen ("great perfection") being the highest. Traditionally, the Nine Vehicles are taught in three versions: as Central, Northern, and Southern treasures. The Central treasure is closest to Nyingma Nine Yānas teaching and the Northern treasure is lost. Tenzin Wangyal[20] Rinpoche elaborated the Southern treasure with shamanism.

According to the Southern Treasure, the nine vehicles and the Four Portals and Treasury are described in the table below. Note information from the following tables originates in:

> http://shenten.org/yungdrung-bon/77-history
> https://en.wikipedia.org/wiki/Tonpa_Shenrab_Miwoche

---

[20] "Tenzin Wangyal Rinpoche."

The Nine Ways of Bon in the Southern Treasure			
The Vehicle		Meaning	Classification
The Way of Prediction	Chashen	Codifies ritual, prognostication, sortilege, and astrology divination, examination of causes	Casual Way/Vehicles
The way of the Visual World	Nangshen	Visible Manifestation expounds the origin and nature of gods and demons living in this world and various methods of exorcism and ransom.	Casual Way/Vehicles
The Way of Illusion	Trulshen	Magical Powers explain the rites for the dispersal of adverse tulpas, entities, and energies	Casual Way/Vehicles
The Way of Existence	Sishen	Deals with the after-death state (Bardo) and with methods for guiding sentient beings towards liberation or at least towards a better rebirth.	Casual Way/Vehicles
The Way of a Lay Follower [Virtuous Lay Practitioners]	Genyen	Contains the ten principles for wholesome activity; guides those who apply the ten virtues and ten perfections.	Resultant Way/Vehicles
Way of a Monk [Sage]	Drangsong	Contains/codifies the rules of monastic discipline.	Resultant Way/Vehicles
The Way of Primordial Sound [Way of the White]	Akar	Charts the integration of an exalted practitioner into the mandala of highest enlightenment;	Resultant Way/Vehicles
Way of the Primordial Shen	Yeshen	Stresses the need for a suitable teacher, place, and occasion for Tantric practices explains the mandala in greater detail as well as instructions for deity meditation.	Resultant Way/Vehicles
Way of Supreme Natural Condition [Way of Great Perfection]	Lame	Concerned with the highest attainment through the path of Great Perfection, Dzogchen	Way of Dzogchen

The Four Portals and the Treasury, the Fifth the Treasury			
The Four Portals		Meaning	
White Water	chab dkar	Contains spells and higher esoteric Tantric practices	
Black Water	chab nag	It consists of various rituals healing, purification, magical, prognostication, divinatory, funerary, and ransom rituals.	
Land of Phan	'Phan yul	Explains rules for monks and nuns and laypeople and expounds philosophical doctrines.	
Divine Guide	dpon gsas	Instructs on psycho-spiritual exercises and meditation practices of Great Perfection - Dzogchen teachings	
Treasury	mtho thog	Serves as an anthology of the salient items of the Four Portals.	

The shaman sees and works with raw, natural elements, regardless of whether they are good or bad. The elements are external to him or her, and each invokes spirits, deities, healing goddesses, and ancestor spirits, all of whom are non-physical beings. The nature of the shaman's involvement is not one of pursuing enlightenment; the shaman focuses on removal of obstacles in a person's life, healing, soul loss or damage, the spirits and confronting and banishing evil spirits, which collectively fall under The Casual Way or Casual vehicles, described in the previous table. The Casual Way or Casual Vehicles create the foundations for the Resultant Way or Resultant Vehicles and, ultimately, the higher levels of sutra, Tantra, and Dzogchen.

In shamanic rituals, symbols play a significant role. The shaman is adept at working with symbols that reflect a connection between this physical, material world, and the realm in which the spirits and deities they are connecting with exist. Food created for an offering may ultimately be left outside a home for animals to consume. The fact they do does not diminish the act of gathering and preparing the offering, not the belief that the offering has value to the spirits and deities. The ceremony in which the offering is presented to the spirits and deities has value as an expression of belief, connection, and value.

The shaman may also use herbal preparations to be ingested as tea or burned so that healing smoke may be inhaled. In addition, the shaman helps by spiritually gathering energies from spirits associated with the five elements, the elements that the receipt is missing. The ultimate goal is to restore harmony and balance within the recipient and the recipient to the environment.

Connecting the raw, natural elements with the corresponding element within us not only connects us to the natural world, in a shamanic view, this connection speaks to the soul.

5.2   Earth Element

In the past, I have gone to a bench close by a large lake; there are plentiful benches to sit and quietly retrospect. In the summer, I will take off my sandals and sit with my bare feet on the ground. As I concentrate on the grounding effect of connecting the earth element under my feet and the earth element within myself, it feels as if the soles of my feet are growing roots into the ground. I am deeply connecting to the earth. I feel the grounding effect move up my legs and give me stability. There have been times when perhaps I should not have taken my shoes, it being too cold for sandals. Still, I put my bare feet on the ground but somehow, it is not cold or wet.

5.3   Water Element

The bench is beside a very large lake. As I sit and watch, I see the turbulent water when the wind is strong, I hear the lake lapping at the shoreline and the rocks. I have been a scuba diver in that lake so I know that even when the surface is turbulent, deeper down the water is still and calm. Water is comforting, even when it is turbulent because it is fascinating to watch. It wraps itself around you and gives a feeling of being solid even when it is flowing all around you. On a calm day, the surface is relaxing and comforting. As we lean back off the dive boat and fall in, it moves around us and accepts us. Bring these qualities into ourselves. Being late for a meeting, being in an argument are not things to upset the element of water within us.

5.4   Fire

That same bench by the lake has allowed me to drink in the warm sunlight. The sunlight, especially early in the morning, gifts a feeling of warmth and energy that soaks in through the skin. If my blood is not warm, it is after it has passed over my hands, arms, legs, and face, which are all turned towards the rising run. There is a sensation within my body that it is being supercharged. Nerves are firing and my heat starts to engage my sense of growth and maturity. I let my mind think about creative things and things I can use my talents and feelings to perfect and grow. There are things that need to be burned away. Relationships that are over but have not "ended" are ended in eth fire of the sun and what it brings within me, as I use that huge fire internally to energize myself. At the end of sitting there and absorbing and internalizing all this energy, I feel as though I have had a spiritual shower.

5.5   Air

The same lake and benches allow me to experience the element air. The lake is 53 miles wide [85 KM] where I am sitting so there is plenty of space, another element, for the winds to gather and blow. I have sat there and seen the wind push the surface of the water element into waves and then blow the tips of the waves in white caps. I watch the birds flying on the air currents and marvel at their mastery of the insubstantial but powerful winds. When the breezes are gentle and mild, they push the water element slightly against the shore line. I bring the lightness and unbounded nature of wind into myself as flexibility that encourages me to move beyond negative thoughts and obstacles, just as the birds fly casually through the winds.

5.6   Space

Because the lake is so large at that point, I cannot see the other side. So, like an ocean, the sky seems bigger than I see out of my windows. It is open, big, clear and blue, and seems to be all around me and dissolve me into it. I am so surprised at how much I can see and feel. Anger, fear, desire, and worry all disappear into the immensity of the sky, the space element. I absorb these feelings into myself; they help me grow and, at the same time, be collected and cool.

I am lucky to have this wonderful resource so close by that I can visit it often. Always thank the elements for being where you have been exploring and absorbing their unique values. In a Buddhist view, giving tanks like this earns merit, not just for giving thanks, but for recognizing, enjoying, and being open and aware to the qualities of the external elements and bringing them within me, to join with the elements in me, and heal and make myself better and help me on my spiritual path.

Focusing on myself though is one part of gathering merit. Also, make a wish, a deeply felt one, that all beings, human or animal, are freed from suffering and can share the bounty I have just received and taken into myself.

5.7   Sentient Being in Each Element

To the shaman, each of the five elements contains independent, living, sentient spirits. They are non-physical beings with whom he can make contact. The spirits may support us, deny us, or be neutral. Purchasing land, buying plants, and caring for a pet all bring us into contact with the spirits of that element or that animal or plant.

When a bird makes a nest in a tree, they are building them. That is where they will bring up their family just as we look to the land with the intent of building our home to raise our family. The bird will fight other birds for the nesting space and their nest. There are insects, fish, and burrowing animals that also look to the land for their home. They will also fight for the right to retain their space and their art of that land.

Cutting down the tree smashes the birds' home, destroys its eggs and kills its young. Bulldozing the ground destroys the burrows of animals that nest underground. Yet these are physical beings we can see and hear, the non-physical beings we do not. Yet they have the ability to hinder the building process or make it go smoothly. A hindrance from the Earth Element might be unexpected problems with the ground, rocks, or underground streams, which indicate the water element is unhappy as well. Disagreements, accidents, or illness in the construction team. If great progress in construction is made and the team is energized and working well together, we can say everything is going smoothly.

To assist with the construction of the house, for example, connecting with, explaining and asking for permission before changing the ground, the trees, and the water and animals in, under and on the land, we have just purchased. And don't forget, a new house consumes space and changes the way the wind blows across the land where we have built. The deities and spirits for these elements will also need to be considered and engaged with.

After we have made the changes we planned, a ritual of thanks can be held quietly by ourselves is very appropriate. Never forget to say thank you to the spirits and deities we have had dealings with.

Developing this sensitivity and appreciation of the elements, deities, and spirits is part of each of our journey to recognize the planet is both alive and it is sacred.

5.8   Eight Classes of Being

In Tibet, beings on each class listed below are known to have characteristic appearance, temperaments, and how they relate to humans.

From:

The Rigpa Shedra[21] and the Chinese Buddhist Encyclopedia[22]

Name	Tibetan Name	Description
Du	Bdud	The four maras (sometimes also translated as 'demons') which create obstacles to practitioners on the spiritual path. It is important to understand that they have no inherent existence and are only created by the mind.
Rakshasa	Srin Po	is a kind of malignant spirit that eats human flesh.
Mamo	Ma Mo	Wrathful feminine deities forming part of Ekadzati's entourage. The mamos are considered to be among the main natural forces, which may respond to human misconduct and environmental misuse by creating obstacles and disease.
Naga	Klu	Serpent Spirits live beneath the surface of the earth or in the water, and in trees or rocks, and are believed to be endowed with magical powers and wealth, as well as being responsible for certain types of illnesses (Wyl. klu'i nad) transmitted to humans.
Ging	Ging	are minor deities who attend to the main deities in some wrathful mandalas. They appear as skeletons who beat a drum, wear a triangular pennant pinned in the middle of their hair, and ear ornaments that look like colourful fans.
Rahula	Sgra gcan 'dzin	The Buddha's son, who also became the tenth of the Sixteen Arhats.
Tsen	btasan	Red spirits that haunt rocks are all male, the spirits of erring monks of earlier times. When they are subdued by a great practitioner, the Tsen often become the guardian of temples, shrines, and monasteries. Red offerings are made to them.
YakSha	gnod Sbyin	The name of a broad class of nature spirits, usually benevolent, who are caretakers of the natural treasures hidden in the Earth and tree roots.

5.9 Four Levels of Guests

In a Shaman's ritual, he/she considers the level of the guests invited to attend a ritual or ceremony; there are guidelines on how to relate to each.

Guest	Description
First Level	• Fully enlightened beings – very powerful • Buddha's and Bodhisattvas • Free of Ignorance • They have perfected the five wisdoms • We do not control these guests • We ask for their blessings
Second Level	• Not fully enlightened but powerful

21 Rigpa Wiki, "Eight Classes of Gods and Demons."
22 Chinese Buddhist Encyclopedia, "Eight Classes of Gods and Demons."

Guest	Description
	• From the God realm, they make up the retinue of the major deities' guardians and dharma protectors
	• They may be from the realm of existence. Such as Angels.
	• Beings representing the planets and celestial bodies
	• Second level guests help with healing.
	• We treat them with respect and honour them
Third Level	• Beings we have karmic connections with
	• Karmic connections can mean friends and also enemies – in this lifetime and in past existence.
	• A connection may also mean something that has to be completed. It could be a duty or obligation to another spirit, by the spirit that is in us. This obligation is often referred to as a Karmic Debt.
Fourth Level	• Guests of compassion
	• They are weaker than we are; they can benefit from our help.
	• In the BON shamanic tradition, it is important to develop compassion as foundation for our practice.

5.10 Making offering to the Guests

In all the religious traditions of Tibet, offerings are made to spiritual, non-physical beings.

The Mandala offering is foundational to Bon and four schools of Tibetan Buddhism and is made to eth first and second level quests.

Other offerings for specific rituals may be Torma, Alcohol, texts, and prayers; these can be especially long prayers or mantras, jewels and precious stones. Also, acceptable is left over food, or food is not prepared or nothing is left over; use of the mind to prepare and gift an imaginary offering is also acceptable.

While we prepare offerings for an important ritual, such as soul retrieval, or healing, we should also not forget to make offerings when everything is going well. Maintaining health, harmony, love, and happiness are important things in our lives. Preparing offerings to sustain spirits and our happy state is important. We do not want blockages to appear; we want to ensure we prevent obstacles from manifesting that may block us tomorrow. If nothing more, we are honouring our protectors and guides.

5.11 Chang-Bu Offering

It is a simple offering made of flour and water. It is called Chang-Bu or a fingerprint Torma.

A shaman may make and use it, but this can also be made by yourself.

Mae the dough so that is not too wet, it must not be sticky. Think of toothpaste; that consistency is a good guide for the consistency of the Torma. If you are male, lightly oil the right hand; if female, oil the left hand.

Roll the dough until it is a fat roll.

Press the dough into the palm of the oiled hand sufficiently hard that the tough will take on all the ridges, seams, and channels of the skin. Make sure the palm is covered as well as the fingers and thumb. The five fingers and thumb represent the five elements; we want to capture the creases of the fingers where they flex and bend.

Touch the dough to any part of the body that needs healing. This draws spiritual attention to that spot; prana follows the attention, since mind and prana always move together. With the attention on a single part of the body, sensation in that part increases.

We can experience this by touching any place on our bodies and putting our attention there. When this is done with the Chang bu, we use our imagination to draw the illness, trauma, or negativity into the dough.

Try to feel a release in that area of the body. Move the Torma to another part of the body that needs healing. When we have finished, we have a substantial symbol of our illnesses, one that is energetically connected to us; this is offered to the third and fourth guests, the beings who may be causing and maintaining the illness.

The intent behind the ritual is not only to remove the influence of the spirit from the body, but also give the spirit something, which is done through the offering. What is given has some of the energetic properties of the illness but it is now in a purer form that will nourish and satisfy the spirit? When it accepts the offering, it leaves the person whom it has afflicted.

After the ritual is finished, the offering is taken outside and thrown in the direction opposite the individual's birth year sign, the direction, it is believed, in which the negative force is most likely to originate. (If you don't know your sign, refer to the chart at the end of this book.)

Traditionally, after a ritual like this, we look for a dream that signifies success, such as a dream of insects, animals, liquid, or other beings or negative substances coming out of the body.

5.12 The Twelve Astrological Signs and their Directions

Your Tibetan Astrological sign is based on the year of your birth and follows a twelve-year cycle based on the Lunar Calendar. [23]

---

[23] moonhoroscope.com/lunar-birthday, "Lunar Birthday."

The duration of one lunar day is from one moonrise to another, and the entire lunar days in the lunar cycle - 29 or 30, depending on the speed of the moon. Since the lunar day does not coincide with sunny days, the lunar day can begin at any time - in the morning, in the afternoon, in the evening or at night. It is important to consider the fact that the lunar day, as a rule, has different durations and sometimes can last only a few hours. The lunar cycle passes through the four main lunar phases: the new moon, the first quarter, the full moon, and the last quarter.

These phases of the moon since ancient times, have been noted in all lunar calendars. The first lunar day is counted from the moment of the new moon.
To determine the opposite direction to the year of your sign, select your sign as 1 [number one], then count to 7 [number 7] that gives you the opposite of your birth sign.

Lunar Calendar	Gregorian Calendar	Tibetan Birth Sign	Direction
1914, 1926, 1938, 1950, 1962, 1974, 1986, 1998, 2010, 2022 and 2034	Feb. 1, 2022 – Jan. 21, 2023	Tiger	East - closer to Northeast
1915, 1927, 1939, 1951, 1963, 1975, 1987, 1999, 2011 and 2023...	Jan. 22, 2023 – Feb. 9, 2024	Hare	East – closer to Southeast
1916, 1928, 1940, 1952, 1964, 1976, 1988, 2000, 2012 and 2024...	Feb. 10, 2024 – Jan. 29, 2025	Dragon	Southeast
1917, 1929, 1941, 1953, 1965, 1977, 1989, 2001, 2013, 2025, 2037...	Jan. 29, 2025 – Feb. 16, 2026	Snake	South - closer to Southeast
1918, 1930, 1942, 1954, 1966, 1978, 1990, 2002, 2014 and 2026...	Feb. 17, 2026 – Feb. 5, 2027	Horse	South - closer to Southwest
1919, 1931, 1943, 1955, 1967, 1979, 1991, 2003, 2015, 2027, 2039 and 2051...	Feb. 6, 2027 – Feb. 25, 2028	Sheep	Southwest
1920, 1932, 1944, 1956, 1968, 1980, 1992, 2004, 2016 and 2028...	Jan. 26, 2028 – Feb. 12, 2029	Monkey	West - closer to Southwest
1921, 1933, 1945, 1957, 1969, 1981, 1993, 2005, 2017 and 2029...	Feb. 13, 2029 – Feb. 2, 2030	Garuda – Chinese = Rooster	West - closer to Northwest
1922, 1934, 1946, 1958, 1970, 1982, 1994, 2006, 2018, 2030 and 2042...	Feb. 3, 2030 – Jan. 22, 2031	Dog	Northwest
1923, 1935, 1947, 1959, 1971, 1983, 1995, 2007, 2019, 2031, 2043...	Jan 23,2031 Feb 0,2032	Pig/boar	North - closer to Northwest
1913, 1925, 1937, 1949, 1961, 1973, 1985, 1997, 2009, 2021, 2033...	Feb. 12, 2021 – Jan. 31, 2022	Elephant – Chinese = Ox	Northeast
1948, 1960, 1972, 1984, 1996, 2008, and 2020	January 25, 2020, to February 11, 2021	Rat	North – Closer to Northeast

6 Bardo

In some schools of Buddhism, Bardo (Classical Tibetan: བར་དོ Wylie: bar do), antarabhava (Sanskrit), or chuu (Japanese: 中有) is an intermediate, transitional, or liminal state between death and rebirth - reincarnation. Reincarnation into another life, as a different being, is the philosophical or religious concept that the non-physical essence of a living being starts a new life in a different physical form or body after biological death. It is also called rebirth or transmigration.[24]

Bardo is a concept which arose soon after the Buddha's passing, with a number of earlier Buddhist groups accepting the existence of such an intermediate state, while other schools rejected it.

In Tibetan Buddhism, Bardo is the central theme of the Bardo Thodol[25]; literally Liberation Through Hearing During the Intermediate State, in the west, Bardo Thodol is known as the Tibetan Book of the Dead.[26] The Tibetan Book of the Dead is a Lamaist book of counsel, probably influenced by Bon shamanism. The Buddhist lama who whispers this sacred text into the dead man's ear is himself, like the tribal shaman, a psychopomp or soul-guide (Tucci, 194) who accompanies the dead person on his difficult path during the forty-nine days of the intermediate state between death and rebirth.[27]

According to Tibetan tradition, after death and before one's next birth, when one's consciousness is not connected with a physical body, one experiences a variety of phenomena. These usually follow a particular sequence of degeneration from just after death, the clearest experiences of reality of which one is spiritually capable, and then proceeding to terrifying hallucinations that arise from the impulses of one's previous unskillful actions. For the prepared and appropriately trained individuals, the Bardo offers a state of great opportunity for liberation, since transcendental insight may arise with the direct experience of reality; for others, it can become a place of danger, as the karmically created hallucinations can impel one into a less than desirable rebirth.[28]

Symbolically, Bardo can describe times when our usual way of life becomes suspended, as, for example, during a period of illness or during a meditation retreat. Such times can prove fruitful for spiritual progress because external constraints diminish. However, they can also present challenges because our less skillful impulses may come to the foreground, just as in the sidpa Bardo.

The concept of antarabhava,[29] an intervening state between death and rebirth, was brought into Buddhism from the Vedic-Upanishadic philosophical tradition, which later developed into Hinduism.

---

[24] Wikipedia, "Reincarnation."
[25] Britannica, "Bardo ThöDol Tibetan Buddhist Text."
[26] Wikipedia, "Bardo."
[27] University of California Press eBook Collection, "The Spiritual Quest," (1982 - 2004).
[28] Wikipedia, "Bardo."
[29] https://www.wisdomlib.org, "Antarabhava, AntarāBhava 2 Definitions."

From the records of early Buddhist schools, it appears that at least six different groups accepted the notion of an intermediate existence: antarabhava, namely, the Sarvastivada, Darstantika, Vatsiputriyas, Sammitiya, Purvasaila, and late Mahisasaka. The first four of these are closely related schools. Opposing them were the Mahasamghika, early Mahisasaka, Theravada, Vibhajyavada and the Sariputra Abhidharma.

After death, the shaman will undertake a journey to the intermediate world and with their guides and helping spirits seek out the soul of the deceased and guide and encourage it to cross over fully, especially if the wandering soul has been affecting the lives of the remaining living relatives or otherwise causing problems.

The shaman may also be asked to help souls and spirits cross over who had no connection to the living but for some reason have connected themselves to the living and causing illness.

Battles and confrontations with evil or dark spirits and souls may be undertaken to help a sick individual or to help the spirt cross over. The shaman's universe includes an upper, middle, and lower realm where spirits exist, along with the spirits of ancestors who must be understood and persuaded to help a soul in its current physical incarnation.

Because of the split and downright antagonism that often exists between those trained in science and those professing particular religions, there is often little study of each other's accounts of religious and psychic phenomena, so books like those mentioned are often not known outside a narrow circle of experts or academic authorities. Yet it is worth noting that Carol Zaleski's book has already spawned a whole academic field of research into the phenomenology of 'otherworldly realities' - there have been several international conferences to date - while Sogyal's book is now used worldwide to help people who are nearing death prepare for their passing over. [30]

My first realization[31] of how important it is to follow a person's consciousness into other realms, in whatever way possible, came twenty years ago during a psychotherapy session with a woman who had survived a major car accident and had gone through a classic NDE during subsequent surgery to save her life. She was still suffering from manifest PTSD symptoms when she consulted me and I decided to regress her to the memory of the accident. Not only did she relive the accident and release much buried trauma held in her body but she also proceeded to re-play the experience of watching herself from above as ambulance men pulled her body from the wreckage. She then saw her body taken to the hospital and undergoing surgery. Next, she felt herself drifting up to a higher realm and meeting with beings of light she recognized as deceased members of her family, who told her that her work on earth was not finished and that she must return. She remembered the pain of coming back into her body. Prior to the regression, she had not 'remembered' any of this. The session profoundly altered her attitude to death and dying. Indeed, what most deeply struck her was the continuity of her consciousness both before and after her 'death' and both in and out of her body.[32]

---

[30] Dr. Roger J. Woolger, "Beyond Death- Transition and the Afterlife."
[31] Ibid.
[32] Ibid.

In Buddhism Some of the earliest references we have to "intermediate existence" are found in the Sarvastivadin text the Mahavibhasa. For instance, the Mahavibhasa indicates a "basic existence," an "intermediate existence," a "birth existence" and "death existence."

The intermediate being who makes the passage in this way from one existence to the next is formed, like every living being, of the five aggregate skandha[33]. Existence is demonstrated by the fact that it cannot have any discontinuity in time and space between the place and moment of death and those of rebirth, and therefore it must be that the two existences belonging to the same series are linked in time and space by an intermediate stage. The intermediate being is the Gandharva, the presence of which is as necessary at conception as the fecundity and union of the parents. Furthermore, the Antaraparinirvayin is an Anagamin who obtains parinirvana during the intermediary existence. As for the heinous criminal guilty of one of the five crimes without interval (Anantara), he passes in quite the same way by an intermediate existence at the end of which he is reborn, necessarily in hell.[34]

What is an intermediate being, and an intermediate existence? Intermediate existence, which inserts itself between existence at death and existence at birth, not having arrived at the location where it should go, cannot be said to be born. Between death - that is, the five skandhas of the moment of death - and arising - that is, the five skandhas of the moment of rebirth - there is found an existence - a "body" of five skandhas - that goes to the place of rebirth. This existence between two realms of rebirth (gati) is called intermediate existence. He cites a number of texts and examples to defend the notion against other schools, which reject it and claim that death in one life is immediately followed by rebirth in the next, without any intermediate state in between the two. Both the Mahavibhasa and the Abhidharmakosa have the notion of the intermediate state lasting "seven times seven days" i.e., 49 days at most. This is one view, though, and there were also others.[35]

6.1 Six bardos in Tibetan Buddhism

From: Bardo, Wikipedia - https://en.wikipedia.org/wiki/Bardo

1. Kyenay Bardo - Skye gnas bar do is the first Bardo of birth and life. This Bardo commences from conception until the last breath, when the mind stream withdraws from the body.

2. Milam Bardo - rmi lam bar do is the second Bardo of the dream state. The Milam Bardo is a subset of the first Bardo. Dream Yoga develops practices to integrate the dream state into Buddhist sadhana.

3. Samten Bardo - bsam gtan bar do is the third Bardo of meditation. This Bardo is generally only experienced by meditators, though individuals may have spontaneous experience of it. Samten Bardo is a subset of the Shinay Bardo.

[33] Wikipedia, "Skandha."
[34] "Bardo."
[35] Ibid.

4. Chikhai Bardo - 'chi kha'i bar do is the fourth Bardo of the moment of death. According to tradition, this Bardo is held to commence when the outer and inner signs presage that the onset of death is nigh, and continues through the dissolution or transmutation of the Mahabhuta until the external and internal breath has completed.

5. Chonyi Bardo - chos nyid bar do is the fifth Bardo of the luminosity of true nature, which commences after the final 'inner breath' Sanskrit: prana, Vayu; Tibetan: rlung. It is within this Bardo that visions and auditory phenomena occur. In the Dzogchen teachings, these are known as the spontaneously manifesting Thodgal Tibetan: thod-rgyal visions.

    Concomitant to these visions, there is a welling of profound peace and pristine awareness. Sentient beings who have not practised during their lived experience and/or who do not recognize the clear light Tibetan: OD gsal at the moment of death are usually deluded throughout the fifth Bardo of luminosity.

6. Sidpa Bardo - srid pa bar do is the sixth Bardo of becoming or transmigration. This Bardo endures until the inner-breath commences in the new transmigrating form determined by the "karmic seeds" within the storehouse consciousness.

Bardo is also the state where Near-Death Experiences [NDE] take place. The fact is that one of the first assertions that almost all visionaries, mystics, journeyers, and NDE survivors make is that their visions are, without question, of actual existent places or worlds, indeed places or worlds that are manifestly of a non-physical order. It is here that the terminology of 'other' or 'invisible' or 'higher' worlds seems inescapable in describing such experiences. To summarize their claims, we have to say that they are positing a referent that is non-physical and yet real. This upsets the materialist, for whom there is only one reality, namely this one, and at this point he/she must either withdraw from the game or recognize that the greatest minds in the Western tradition have had to face this issue and forgo their assumptions of one-dimensional reality.

When Aristotle, following his master Plato, tried to summarize the knowledge of his day, after writing Physics, he was obliged to add another volume, 'beyond' (meta) the realm of physics, which in Greek became the metaphysics. Plato had already designated a Metaxy, or intermediary world, of subtle spiritual forms that were not physical. Indeed, according to the eminent Indian scholar Ananda K. Coomeraswamy, Plato had already been influenced by the teachings of ancient India, for we find Plato's idea clearly expressed in the Hindu Upanishads as follows: There are two states for man - the state in this world and the state in the next; there is also a third state, the state intermediate between these two, which can be likened to the dream [state]. While in the intermediate state, a man experiences both the other states, that of this world and that in the next; and the manner whereof is as follows: when he dies, he lives only in the subtle body, on which are left the impressions samskaras, Skt. Of his past deeds, and of those impressions, is he aware, illumined as they are by the light of the Transcendent Self Atman, Skt.[36]

---

[36] Wikipedia, "Reincarnation."

7   Soul Loss and the Retrieval of the Elemental Energies

I n the Tibetan tradition, there is the notion of "soul loss." Although this is an imbalance of the elements, it is greater than the imbalances suffered in normal life. It is a question of degree. Soul loss is a profound loss of elemental qualities and a condition of extreme imbalance that usually, though not always, is caused by traumatic external situations and beings.[37]

We say that the soul can be stolen by malevolent beings of the eight classes, which are described in section Eight Classes of Being in this book.

These negative, non-physical external beings damage our capacity for positive human qualities.
This usually happens during trauma, such as emotional or physical abuse, an accident, loss of a loved one, assault, rape, incest, divorce, surgery, or wartime experiences. The soul part leaves as a protective mechanism. In indigenous cultures, the soul part is retrieved by a shaman shortly after the trauma. In our culture, people can go their entire lifetime without the soul part. [38]

Someone may also lose part of their soul by giving it to a loved one through a desire to share themselves with another. In some cases, a soul part may be stolen. [39]

Psychologically, this phenomenon is understood in terms of dissociation, and it is a brilliant survival mechanism for the human psyche. The major characteristic of all dissociative phenomena involves a detachment from reality, rather than a loss of reality as in psychosis.[40]

Symptoms of soul loss may include:

- Feeling of incompleteness, or that something is missing

- Feeling like you're not in control of your life

- Feeling like a part of you "died" when something happened.

- Apathy, numbness, lack of vitality or fatigue

- Difficulty staying present in your body or having memory gaps

- Depression

What has been lost can be retrieved by the shaman through the practice and rituals of Soul Retrieval. The ritual is complicated and requires instruction and teaching by qualified master.

---

[37] Tenzin Wangyal Rinpoche, "Soul Retrieval and Related Ideas."
[38] Theinnervoyage.com, "Soul Retrieval."
[39] Ibid.
[40] Wikipedia, "Dissociation Psychology."

The shaman first needs to speak to and understand the recipient of the soul retrieval. He or she needs to understand what is missing and what has been damaged so that they may undertake the soul retrieval ritual. Some will call this a diagnosis.

During the ritual, the shaman will enter an altered state of consciousness or ASC. This may be achieved by dance, rhythmic drumming, plant-based hallucinogens or alcohol. However, not all shamans use these techniques; each shaman is unique and uses different techniques to reach the state they need to soul journey.

During the soul journey, the Shaman will join with either a main helping spirit or a series of spirits that will aid in the search for the soul, which may be more fragmented. At this point in the ritual, the shaman and helping spirts must determine the state of the soul and/or its fragments and what healing needs to be undertaken before it is given back to the recipient. It also needs to be determined if the souls or fragments are being held hostage by a spirit and what the intention of that spirit is.

The shaman negotiates with the hostage taker in order to get back the soul or piece they are holding on to. A special, separate ritual may have to be completed in order to satisfy the hostage taker. In some situations, a struggle may be undertaken by the shaman and their helping spirits and the hostage taker to pull back the soul or otherwise free the soul.

In all the activity of searching and possibly struggling with a spirit, the shaman must protect his or her own spirit. Ensure it remains intact and is not damaged by the actions undertaken. The strength of the helping spirits and experience of the shaman in preforming soul retrieval is essential to the success of the ritual.

Once the shaman and their helping spirits have gathered the soul and any fragments and have healed them, they must be returned to the recipient. The traditional reintegration of the soul with the recipient's physical being is through breath. The shaman breathes hard at or on the recipient and matches the intensity with the intention of sending the soul back to them, and focusing on returning their light. The soul or soul fragments at this stage are like lost children being returned to their parents.

Then we support the client to begin the process of integrating this new energy, by first just allowing the energy to sink down into their bones and cells, which go deeply into the recipient.

7.1   Element Retrieval

As with soul retrieval, the elemental energy of a recipient may be lost, stolen or so seriously unbalanced it may appear that a p [articular element has been taken away.
Sutra, Tantra, and the shamanic vehicles include practices to reconnect us to the positive qualities. This process is not just about having pleasant experiences; it is about connecting to deeper aspects of ourselves. Although ultimately, we need to go beyond the simplicity of positive and negative, until we actually do, positive qualities lead us closer to the experience of the base of existence, while negative qualities distract us and lead further into abstraction.[41]

_____
[41] Tenzin Wangyal Rinpoche, "Tibetan Soul Retrieval."

When elemental qualities are lost, there is a flattening of experience, a loss of richness and resonance. This is similar to the experience of a broken heart. A man or woman loses a spouse or partner in a shocking way, is betrayed or abandoned, and he or she closes the heart. This is a familiar theme in novels and movies: the person can't love because of the fear of being hurt again. The same kind of inner damage can happen when someone loses a child, is raped, witness's brutality, is subjected to brutality, goes through a war, is in a car accident, or loses a house – the catastrophes and calamities that fall upon us humans. The shock to the soul overwhelms it with fear, loss, or some other powerful emotion and, and the result is the loss of positive qualities, the loss of life force and vitality and the loss of joy and empathy. It may also result in physical frailty and the loss of sensory clarity.[42]

Regardless of whether the loss of elemental energy is sudden or occurs over time, or is the result of a traumatizing or dehumanizing environment, the damage to the energy of the elements and their balance in the recipient. The cause is a negative spirit, or spirits.

When we are physically weakened, our physical body is susceptible to bacterial and virus infections from bacteria and viruses. When we are psychically weakened, we are susceptible to the influences of negative non-physical beings.

After an accident, for instance, an individual may experience lethargy, a loss of inspiration and creativity, or a loss of vigour. This condition may heal naturally, but if it doesn't, if fire element energy has been lost, it can become chronic. This may show up in work and in relationships, and may manifest in the body as an illness and in the mind as a disturbance in cognitive activity. The accident is the apparent physical cause of the loss, but the real loss is caused by trauma or can come as the person is weakened and vulnerable to malevolent external beings. In either case, the damage is manifested in the soul.[43]

Element retrieval also refers to the overabundance of an element which causes spiritual imbalance. The shaman must soul journey to discover the source of the abundance and remove it, and, after removing it, the shaman must rebalance the elements and manage any damage done by the time there was the overabundance of the element. If someone is too grounded as a result of the imbalance, the shaman must support the elements of Air and Space, for example.

7.2   Blocked or closed chakras.

Depending on the impact to us by events such as being betrayed by a lover, the loss of a loved one or a parent and a physical accident, one or more of our chakras may have become blocked or restricted. If you sit quietly, eyes closed, warm, comfortable and breathing normally. No external distractions. Clear your mind and let all distracting thoughts pass. Feel your quietness.

---

[42] "Soul Retrieval and Related Ideas."
[43] Ibid.

Rituals to unblock or remove restrictions in a recipient's chakras may be carried out to return the strength and vibrancy of the chakras affected. This also requires the shaman to engage in balancing and ensuring a clear flow of energy from the root to the crown chakra.

7.3   Divination

In traditional Tibetan culture, when people begin to suffer from this kind of condition, they ask for a divination. Divination is considered an important means to diagnose the source of energy disturbances and to indicate what can be done to heal those disturbances. Divination sometimes suggests the need for a soul retrieval. In other cases, even without divination, people may feel that a soul retrieval is warranted.[44]

---

[44] Ibid.

8   Persecution of Shaman

8.1   Religious Persecution in Tibet

Current religious persecution in Tibet does not stem from ethnic or religious conflict or discrimination by a majority against a minority. It is politically motivated, and consciously applied to realize political and military ends.

8.2   History

The Tibetan Plateau has been inhabited by humans for at least 21,000 years. The Neolithic period saw immigrants from northern China largely displace the humans around 3,000 years ago. There remains some genetic continuity between the Paleolithic inhabitants and contemporary Tibetan populations.[45]

The earliest Tibetan historical texts identify the Zhang Zhung culture as a people who migrated from the Amdo region into what is now the region of Guge in western Tibet. Zhang Zhung is considered to be the original home of the Bon religion.

By the 1st century BCE – Before Common Era[46], a neighbouring kingdom arose in the Yarlung Valley, and the Yarlung king, Drigum Tsenpo, attempted to remove the influence of the Zhang Zhung by expelling the Zhang's Bon priests from Yarlung. He was assassinated and Zhang Zhung continued its dominance of the region until it was annexed by Songtsen Gampo in the 7th century. Prior to Songtsen Gampo, the kings of Tibet were more mythological than factual, and there is insufficient evidence of their existence.

The fall of the Tibetan Empire[47] resulted in the region breaking up into a variety of territories each controlled by a warlord with overall influence being either Mongol or Chinese but with a reasonable amount of self-determination and flexibility. Eventually, with the fall of the Mongol empire and influence, Tibet was absorbed into the Chinese provinces of Sichuan and Qinghai. Generally, the current borders of Tibet were determined by the 18th century.

In 1950, The Peoples Republic of China negotiated an agreement with the newly enthroned 14th Dalai Lama affirming China's sovereignty over Tibet. Autonomy Created the Tibetan Autonomous Regional [TAR] and the head of the government to be ethnic Tibetan. In reality, the actual power in the TAR is the First Secretary of the Tibetan Autonomous Regional Committee of the Chinese Communist Party, who has never been a Tibetan. The role of ethnic Tibetans in the higher levels of the TAR Communist Party remains very limited.

In exile, the Dalai Lama[48] repudiated the agreement. Many Tibetans have fled Tibet to Nepal and India. The Dalai Lama has a strong following; many Tibetans look at him as both a political and a spiritual leader.

---

[45] Wikipedia, "Tibet."
[46] "Common Era."
[47] "Tibetan Empire."
[48]

A rival Tibetan government-in-exile, The Central Tibetan Administration, also referred to as The Tibetan Government in Exile, is located in India. Its internal structure is government-like; it has stated that it is "not designed to take power in Tibet"; rather, it will be dissolved as soon as freedom is restored in Tibet in favour of a government formed by Tibetans inside Tibet. In addition to political advocacy, it administers a network of schools and other cultural activities for Tibetans in India. [49]

During the Chinese Cultural Revolution[50] 1959-1961 most of Tibet's more than 6,000 monasteries were destroyed and others severely damaged and defaced by the Communist Party of China and monastic estates were broken up and secular education introduced.[51] During this period, religious objects, of any sort, were confiscated and destroyed, removing a significant amount of personally owned history and connection with the past heritage of Tibet.

Restrictions were lifted during the 1980s as a result of a period of relative accommodation but it resulted in a resurgence of religious activity both formal and public as well as personal; Tibetans created altars in their homes, prayed in public, and made pilgrimages to holy places. Rebuilding of temples and monasteries - almost entirely supported by people's voluntary labour and resources. Those monasteries and nunneries were filled with young monks and nuns who wished to pursue a religious vocation in spite of growing up under Communist Chinese rule.

In 1987 and subsequent years, the arrest of monks, nuns, and the display of images of the Dali Lama, shouting slogans and putting up posters have been instituted. Subsequent economic and other reforms have sought to suppress religious activity and any visible refence to the Dali Lama as a spiritual or political head of Tibet.

8.3   Shamans

Shamanism is the oldest religious activity in humanity; it was and has been effected in two ways.

First, in a community, a Shaman is a highly respected and honoured confident, healer, and leader. In both Soviet Russia and China, those roles can be manipulated into a portrayal of the shaman as an oppressor of this tribe, or community. They were seen to fall into the same classification as land owners, merchants, local leaders, or aristocracy. In both Soviet Russia and China, Shamans were purged, arrested, tortured, and shot along with the other classes of people communist forces saw as being oppressors and inhibiting progress of socialist ideas and disrupting the agricultural and societal changes they wanted to make in the name of state ownership.

Suppression by the Red Army and the People's Liberation Army [China] included not just the shaman, but possessions, all things that formed the shaman's heritage and places of worship. And performance of rituals. Some interesting workarounds to survive the persecution have been recorded. One Shaman in Siberia turned his rituals into what he called a "theatre

---

[49] Wikipedia, "Central Tibetan Administration."
[50] "Cultural Revolution."
[51] Ibid.

production." In this way, he was providing entertainment rather than say a soul retrieval ritual, if anyone from the local Soviet happened to be in the "audience" and wanted to know. Other Shamans survived by simply being in very remote locations that the communist re-educators and military did not care to go.

In both Soviet Russia and Tibet, the systematic state sponsored destruction of monasteries and arrest of monks and nuns was material to deprive their respective societies of the physical presence of shamans, Bonpo, and Buddhist monks as well as the physical presence of buildings and places of worship.

The heritage and substance of shamanism, which had been part of a chain of religious growth, through Bon and ultimately into Tibetan Buddhism with its scholarly monastic environment where practices and beliefs were recorded in books and scripture, was unlike any persecution that had come and gone previously.

The introduction of Russian and Chinese languages with state education to replace shamanic teachings and monastic education has resulted in more than one generation growing up without any connection to traditional shamanic teaching, training, and practices, or monastic Buddhist teachings. However, as noted previously, this did not prevent people of all ages attempting reconnection with their spiritual and religious heritage.

Since the collapse of the Soviet system in 1991, there has been a resurgence of Shamanic activity in The Mongolian People's Republic. To the point where Shamans advertise, they can be members of the Corporate Union of Mongolian Shamans, appear on television and run for local administrative political positions.
However, the loss of people, Shamans, men and women who provided a physical presence and their oral history along with their costumes, drums, altars, and all their paraphernalia cannot be replaced, just as the heritage in the monasteries destroyed by the Chinese communists cannot be replaced.

There are two key differences between the resurgence of Shamanism in Mongolia and Tibet. First, Mongolia is free to determine its own path, and make its own laws and regulations. Second is the deep and magnetic reverence for Chinggis Khan, or Genghis Khan,[52] and the achievement of the Mongol people during the Mongolian Empire is genuine and a source of pride and self-identity.

8.4   Current Threats

Persecution in Soviet Russia and Communist China was systematic, organized, and state sponsored. Shamanism faces new forms of denigration and persecution.

Changes are needed to Western notions of shamanism, the shamanic healer, and the role of altered states of consciousness (ASC). Before the Age of Enlightenment, the shaman was condemned as demoniac charlatan. From the mid-19th until the mid-20th century, the shaman was generally considered as being afflicted with a psychiatric or epileptic condition;

---

[52] Wikipedia, "Genghis Khan."

a notion based on the misinterpretation of altered states of consciousness in shamanic rituals as psychopathological. [53]

It is worth noting at this point that the shaman is not possessed. Shamanism is not a possession-based belief. Shamanic possession is not actually possession at all, but the intentional embodiment of spirit helps with whom the shaman has already developed a working relationship. Possession is unintentional intrusion of a foreign spirit into a person, which is considered an energetic illness or unhealthy state in shamanism. Embodiment is an effective, working, altered state the shaman is able to begin and end at will.

Shamanism and possession nonetheless share biological features in their elicitation of ancient brain systems to modify consciousness in relation to healing and spiritual experiences.

The word shaman has been misapplied to other indigenous healers. This was covered in detail in the first book of The Practical Shaman series. A Shaman is not a Witch Doctor, nor is the Shaman a Medicine Man/Woman.

Neoshamanism refers to "new" forms of shamanism, or methods of seeking visions or healing. Neoshamanism comprises an eclectic range of beliefs and practices that involve attempts to attain altered states and communicate with a spirit world. Neoshamanic systems may not resemble traditional forms of shamanism. Some have been invented by individual practitioners, though many borrow or gain inspiration from a variety of different indigenous cultures. In particular, indigenous cultures of the Americas have been influential. [54]

Neoshamanism is not a single, cohesive belief system, but a collective term for many philosophies and activities. However, certain generalities may be drawn between adherents. Most believe in spirits and pursue contact with the "spirit world" in altered states of consciousness, which they achieve through drumming, dance, or the use of entheogens. Most systems might be described as existing somewhere on the animism/pantheism spectrum. Some neoshamans are not trained by any traditional shaman or member of any American indigenous culture, but rather learn independently from books and experimentation. Many attend New Age workshops and retreats, where they study a wide variety of ideas and techniques, both new and old.[55]

Some members of traditional, indigenous cultures and religions are critical of neoshamanism, asserting that it represents an illegitimate form of cultural appropriation, or that it is nothing more than a ruse by fraudulent spiritual leaders to disguise or lend legitimacy to fabricated, ignorant, and/or unsafe elements in their ceremonies.

According to York (2001), one difference between neoshamanism and traditional shamanism is the role of fear. Neoshamanism and its New Age relations tend to dismiss the existence of evil, fear, and failure. "In traditional shamanism, the shaman's initiation is an ordeal involving

---

[53] Wolfgang G. Jilek, "Transforming the Shaman Changing Western Views of Shamanism and Altered States of Consciousness."
[54] Wikipedia, "Neoshamanism."
[55] Ibid.

pain, hardship, and terror. New Age, by contrast, is a religious perspective that denies the ultimate reality of the negative, and this would devalue the role of fear as well.'[56]

Inaccurate representation, misrepresentation and careless referencing, attributing actions and belief systems to what is truly a shaman are a danger to shamans everywhere.

---

[56] Ibid.

9   Shaman Costume

n book one, we covered the core of the shaman's costume; Head Band and Head Dress, Cloak, Footwear, alters and shines

9.1 Mirrors

The traditional costume of a Shaman in Siberia, Mongolia, and Tibet includes metal discs, often 15 – 20 centimetres in diameter. The disks are shiny and tied to the costume through a hole in the middle. The disks are mirrors.

Ceremonial mirrors date back to Neolithic times with the art of grinding and polishing stone. Obsidian and jade were often used in ancient mirrors, and these stones are found in different locations around the world, such as Mexico, Anatolia, and China. Polished, iron-rich meteorites may also predate cast bronze mirrors, and these have been used for a very long time in Tibet to create mirrors and other sacred objects.[57]

Today the mirrors are made of modern metals, steel, copper, or tin. Actual glass mirrors are not used because they can break, or be broken. The oldest mirrors are from China and can be thousands of years old and those are made from bronze.

China is an ancient civilization and has a great influence on the broader region; Korea and Japan to the east, Tibet and Central Asia to the west, and Siberia to the north. This influence included many of the shamanic and magical practices of these regions.

Use of ceremonial bronze mirrors in China can be traced back 4,000 years. They are generally round, have a central raised knob on the back with a hole in it, and decoration on the non-reflective side. The high point of Chinese mirror making was from the start of the Han (206 BCE - 220 CE) to the end of the Tang Dynasties (618 - 907 CE), and many shaman's mirrors date back to these periods, although new mirrors have been continually made up to the present day.[58]

These mirrors are considered magical, and are part of the shaman's armour. It is worn or attached to their costume over the heart, protecting it. A second mirror is attached to the costume at the back, in the same place so that the shaman's heart cannot be attacked from behind.

The shiny side is worn facing outwards. The goal is to ward off evil and malevolent spirits the shaman may encounter in this world or the others to which he journeys. An evil spirit approaching the shaman will see their face reflected back at them in the mirror and flee in terror, leaving the shaman untouched. For this reason, glass mirrors are unsuitable, as the evil spirit may find a way to break the glass, leaving the shaman unprotected. The back of the mirror is concave and focuses light into a central spot, increases the energy. It is worn with this side facing the body to increase personal wind horse energy.[59]

---

[57] https://www.greenshinto.com, "Zen, Shinto and Shaman Mirrors."
[58] SacredHoop.org, "Mirrors of the Soul."
[59] Ibid.

The mirrors have played an important part in traditional Feng Shui, where they are used to reflect negative influences, and alter the shapes of things to increase positive influences.[60]

These magical mirrors are frequently found as grave goods in archeological digs. They had a major role in ancient Chinese death traditions, where a mirror was often placed on the dead person's chest as a 'heart protecting mirror' to keep the person safe on their journey to the next world, and wall paintings in Chinese tombs show people holding up mirrors faced outward, to frighten spirits away.

In many parts of Asia, where shamans have given up the full traditional shaman's attire, they continue to wear at least one mirror.

Mirrors have different names depending on the region the shaman comes from, for instance, they are called *toli* in Mongolia, *panaptu* in Manchuria and *melong* in Tibet.

They may be used in a number of other ways other than to reflect the image of evil and malevolent spirits. Depending on the location and the heritage of shamanistic practices, they may be used for seeing into other worlds, divination, as astrological charms, and for looking into the future. To look into the future, the shaman uses the shiny side. To look into the past, the concave side is used.

When used in healing practices, the shaman looks at a reflection of the sick person to determine their illness and healing required.[61] The mirror may be used to store healing energy; the sick person looks into the mirror to receive the energy.

To dispel troublesome mental states, a person may hold a hand mirror at arm's length, with the shiny side facing away from them. Focusing their mind on the back of the mirror and the concave side, they visualize their problems leaving them and passing through the centre of the concave side. The shiny side "broadcasts" their troubles and does not allow them to return.
They may be simple, undecorated discs of metal, or they may be decorated on one or both sides with Buddhist astrological symbols or Buddhist images. The back or concave side may have animals, plants, or deities in low relief.

They are sometimes made from a special blend of eight medals; gold, silver, mercury, copper, nickel, tin, iron (sometimes from meteorites) and lead, but more commonly are simply brass or silver.[62]

Worn attached to a costume, on a cord or leather strap wound the neck, as a pendant, earrings or as hand mirror, the purpose is always the same.

Large mirrors displayed on altars are called "alter mirrors" and are displayed openly. If it is a Buddhist altar, the mirror, or mirrors symbolize radiant emptiness. If it is a shamanic altar, the mirror, or mirrors are homes for helper spirits and symbols of shamanic power. Alter mirrors are also used in Shinto and Zen ceremonies and alters.

---

[60] Ibid.
[61] Ibid.
[62] Ibid.

9.2   Ribbons

The Shaman's costume displays multicoloured ribbons. These ribbons represent the colours of the five sacred elements and are displayed in the same order as prayer flags.

Traditionally, prayer flags come in sets of five: one in each of five colours. The colours are arranged from left to right in a specific order: blue, white, red, green, and yellow. The five colours represent the five elements and the Five Pure Lights. Different elements are associated with different colours for specific traditions, purposes, and sadhana.[63]

Colour	Symbolizes
Blue	Sky and Space
White	Air and Wind
Red	Fire
Green	Water
Yellow	Earth

---

[63] Wikipedia, "Prayer Flag."

10 Asian and European Shamanism

10.1 Hmong Shamanism

The Hmong are an ancient Chinese people they have a history going back over 5,000 years. Today they continue their Ua Neeb shamanic practices. To a Hmong shaman, there is their main job, their reason for existence and the soul path purpose they were destined to follow. Their rituals and beliefs invoke trance to bring harmony to the individual, family, and community.

At the end of the Vietnam War, 200,000 Hmong were resettled in the United States and continued to practise shamanism there. The Hmong practice animal sacrifice as part of their shamanic rituals. Animal sacrifice has been part of their rituals for over 5,000 years. Animal sacrifice is not a brutal killing a helpless animal; the sacrificial animals and the process of taking life are treated with great respect and care. However, animal sacrifice is not part of American life and as a result The Hmong have found themselves in a number of court cases and friction with authorities as a result.

The Hmong believes that all things on Earth have a soul, or multiple souls. The souls are equal and interchangeable. Sickness is believed to be the result of a person's soul being lost or captured by a wild spirit; the animal to be sacrificed is asked to give up its soul in exchange for that of the suffering individual. This is to be for 12 months. During the Hmong New Year ceremonies, the shaman performs a ritual to release the soul of that animal, where it is sent to the world beyond and the soul is also reincarnated at a higher level or even becomes part of God's family and lives a life of luxury, free of animal suffering. Undertaking this sacrifice and service is a very high honour for the animal.

Hmong shaman also attempt to treat physical illnesses through use of sacred words - khawv koob.

10.2 Japan

Shamanism is part of the indigenous Ainu religion and, more broadly, Shinto. Shinto is distinct in that its shamanism is for an agricultural society.

From the Early Middle Ages, Shinto has been influenced by religious practices from East Asian shamanism or Shintoism. Most particularly, it has been affected by Buddhism.

10.3 S. Korea

Shamanism is still practised in North and South Korea.

In South Korea, shamans are almost entirely female. The name for an S. Korean Shaman is Mudang; male shamans are referred to as baksoo mudang. A person can become a shaman through hereditary title or through natural ability.

Shamans are consulted in contemporary society for financial and marital decisions. As noted in book 1 of this series, S. Korean Mudangs are highly costumed and rituals are performed both privately and as a theatrical performance. Mudangs are accompanied by musicians, singers and often a stage or platform on which the ritual is performed for a usually seated audience.

10.4 Malaysia

Shamanism is practised by the Malay community on the Malay Peninsula and by indigenous people in Sabah and Sarawak.

People who practise shamanism in the country are generally called bomoh or pawang in the Peninsula. In Sabah, the Bobohizan is the main shaman among the Kadazan-Dusun indigenous community.

10.5 Mongolia

Mongol Shamans historically and today may be male or female and fill many roles in Mongol society. Exorcisms, healers, rainmakers, oneiromancers, soothsayers, and as members of the Corporate Union of Mongolian Shamans, run for public office, they appear on television and radio, and advertise their services.

As a member of the Mongolian Shamans Association, they can participate in the continued revival of Mongolian Shamanism.

Historically, the clan based Mongol society was complex and the spirit world matched the physical world in its complexity.

The highest spirit group was the 99 Tngri; Fifty-five being benevolent or "white" and 44 terrifying or "black." White and black banners we raised in all Mongolian encampments and both honoured. Because of their fierceness, the black banner and its 44 Tngri rode into any battles the clan or the greater Mongols fought. It was the banner under which Chinggis Khan[64] built the Mongol Empire. It is worth noting that Chinggis Khan, though not a shaman, worshipped and interceded with the black Tngri frequently during his lifetime. The Tngri were followed by 77 natigai or "earth mothers." Mongolian shamanism incorporates ancestor worship. Chief of the ancestors a shaman may call on are the closely connected wand those by groups of ancestral spirits the "Lord-Spirits" these being the spirits and souls of clan leaders who will provide physical and spiritual help. Next are "Protector-Spirits" these being the souls and spirits of great shamans, male and female. Lesser shamans [male and female] were called "Guardian-Spirits," which were connected to a specific locality, such as a mountain or river belonging to the clan.

In the 1990s, the Soviet system fell. There has been a considerable growth in shamanism and many, many more shamans have appeared. As members of the Corporate Union of Mongolian Shamans or Mongolian Shamans Association, a modernization of the role of shamans has taken place. Some Mongolian shamans are now making a business out of their

---

[64] "Genghis Khan."

profession and even have offices in the larger towns. At these businesses, a shaman generally heads the organization and performs services such as healing, fortune-telling, and solving all kinds of problems.

This has led traditional shamans amongst the Buryat Mongols to struggle to re-establish their historical and genetic roots now that Soviet oppression has been lifted.

Another dynamic has been a gradual change in the openness of Mongol shamans to offer insights into the role of a shaman. Seeking to protect their ethnic connection and the basis of their practices. Many organizations such as those mentioned are reticent, even restricting access from western neo and New Age shamans.

10.6 Philippines

Babaylans[65], were shamans of ethnic groups of the pre-colonial Philippine islands. They were highly respected in the community being elevated to the status of a pre-colonial noble class.

They specialized in harnessing the unlimited powers of nature and were almost always women or feminized men. They were believed to have spirit guides, by which they could contact and interact with the spirits of the spirit world.

They acted as mediums during rituals and specialized in various practices such as healing, herbalism, divination, or sorcery. They were reputed to be able to bring down an enemy, hence their reputation with divine combat.

Gradual conversion to Islam and the later Spanish colonial forced conversion to Catholicism reduced their influence. They were persecuted vigorously by the Spanish, who burned and destroyed anything associated with indigenous religion and murdered thousands of practitioners.

10.7 Siberia and North Asia

Siberia, north of the Mongols – see Mongolia in this section, is inhabited by many different ethnic groups who observe shamanistic practices. Many classical ethnographic sources of shamanism were recorded among Siberian peoples.

Manchu Shamanism[66] [67] is one of very few shamanist traditions which held official status into the modern era, by becoming one of the imperial cults of the Qing dynasty of China, together with Buddhism, Taoism and traditional Heavenly worship. The Palace of Earthly Tranquility[68] is one of the principal halls of the Forbidden City[69] in Beijing and was partly dedicated to shamanistic rituals. The ritual set-up is still preserved in situ today.

---

[65] "Babaylan."
[66] "Manchu Shamanism."
[67] "Shamanism in the Qing Dynasty."
[68] "Palace of Earthly Tranquility."
[6969] "Forbidden City.Pdf."

Amongst the Siberian Chukchi[70] people, a shaman is selected by the spirits. The candidate is possessed by a spirit that demands they assume the role of shaman. The Buryat have a ritual known as shanar whereby a candidate is consecrated as shaman by another, already-established shaman.

Among several Samoyedic[71] peoples, shamanism is a living tradition also in modern times, especially at groups living in isolation, until recent times.

---

[70] "Chukchi People."
[71] "Samoyedic Peoples."

Linguistic Family[72]	Peoples	Shamanism
Uralic	Samoyedic	Among several Samoyedic people's shamanism was a living tradition into modern times, especially at groups living in isolation until recent times. There were distinguished several types of shamans among Nenets, Enets, and Selkup people. The Nganasan shaman used three different crowns, according to the situation: one for the upper world, one for underneath word and one for the occasion of childbirth.
	Nenets	Several types of shamans distinguished by the world they connected with; upper world, underworld, or the dead
	Nganasan	The last notable shaman rituals and seance were performed and recorded in the 1970's
	Sayan Samoyedic	In the 19th century, a language shift saw the adoption of the neighbouring Turkic People. Today the original language is extinct. Karagas Shamanism is influenced by Abakan-Turkic and Buryat practices and Khalkha Mongol,[73] is the largest subgroup of Mongol people.

Closure of the border between Soviet Russia and the People's Republic of China in 1949 sealed many nomadic Tungus groups, including the Evenki that practised shamanism in Manchuria and Inner Mongolia. The last shaman of the Oroqen, Chuonnasuan (Meng Jinfu), died in October 2000.

---

[72] "Regional Forms of Shamanism."
[73] "Khalkha Mongols."

10.8 Vietnam

In Vietnam, shamans conduct rituals in many of the religious traditions that co-mingle in the majority and minority populations. In their rituals, music, dance, special garments and offerings are part of the performance that surrounds the spirit journey.

Shamanism is part of the Vietnamese religion of worship of mother goddesses. In Vietnam, this ritual practice is called Len dong or also known as hau bong. Hau bong sessions involve artistic elements such as music, singing, dance and the use of costumes.

Hat châu van, from northern Vietnam, is a traditional folk art of northern Vietnam, related to shamanism. The genre is famous for its use in rituals for deity mediumship. Châu van serves two purposes: to help hypnotize the medium for the reception of the deities, and to accompany the medium's actions with appropriate music.

10.9 Other Asian traditions

Jhakri is the common name used for shamans in Sikkim (India) and Nepal.

They exist in many communities. They are influenced by Hinduism, Tibetan Buddhism, Mun and Bon rites.

Shamanism is still widely practised in the Ryukyu Islands Okinawa, Japan, where shamans are known as 'Noro' all women and 'Yuta.' 'Noro' generally administers public or communal ceremonies, while 'Yuta' focuses on civil and private matters. Shamanism is also practised in a few rural areas in Japan proper. It is commonly believed that the Shinto religion is the result of the transformation of a shamanistic tradition into a religion. Forms of practice vary somewhat in the several Ryukyu islands, so that there is, for example, a distinct Miyako shamanism. [48]
Shamanist practices seem to have been preserved in the Catholic religious traditions of aborigines in Taiwan. [74]

_____

[74] "Regional Forms of Shamanism."

10.10 Europe

Some of the prehistoric peoples who once lived in Siberia and other parts of Central and Eastern Asia migrated into other regions, bringing their cultures with them. For example, many Uralic peoples live outside Siberia; however, the original location of the Proto-Uralic peoples and its extent are debated.

Combined phytogeographical and linguistic considerations, such as the distribution of various tree species, and their names in various Uralic languages, suggest that this area was north of Central Ural Mountains and on lower and middle parts of the Ob River. Newer studies suggest an origin in Northeast Asia.

It is suggested the Proto-Uralic language is linked to the Chinese Liao civilization. The ancestors of Hungarian people or Magyars have wandered from their ancestral proto-Uralic area to the Pannonian Basin. Shamanism played an important role in Turko-Mongol mythology.

Tengriism, the major ancient belief among Xiongnu, Mongol and Turkic peoples, Magyars, and Bulgars, incorporates elements of shamanism. There are no practising shamans in current-day Hungary, but their folklore does make refence to shamans.[75]

For more detailed overview of Regional forms of Shamanism and regions not covered here, please refer to Wikipedia at this link: URL:
https://en.wikipedia.org/wiki/Regional_forms_of_shamanism

---

[75] "Shamanistic Remnants in Hungarian Folklore."

Bibliography:

Britannica. "Bardo ThöDol Tibetan Buddhist Text."

Collection, University of California Press eBook. "The Spiritual Quest." (1982 - 2004).

Encyclopedia, Chinese Buddhist. "Eight Classes of Gods and Demons."

https://www.energy-shifter.com/shamanism-and-spiritual-techniques.html. "Shamanism, and
        Soul Retrieval - Spiritual House Cleansing."

https://www.greenshinto.com. "Zen, Shinto and Shaman Mirrors."

https://www.wisdomlib.org. "Antarabhava, AntarāBhava 2 Definitions."

Jilek, Wolfgang G. "Transforming the Shaman, Changing Western Views of Shamanism and
        Altered States of Consciousness."

Lichtenstein, A. H., A. Berger, and M. J. Cheng. "Definitions of Healing and Healing
        Interventions across Different Cultures." *Ann Palliat Med* 6, no. 3 (Jul 2017): 248-52.

moonhoroscope.com/lunar-birthday. "Lunar Birthday."

Rinchen Yönsiyebü. "White, Black and Yellow Shamans among the Mongols." *Ultimate Reality
        and Meaning* 4, no. 2 (1981): 94-102.

Rinpoche, Tenzin Wangyal. "Soul Retrieval and Related Ideas."

———. "Tibetan Soul Retrieval."

SAAMI, HELEN. "The Khanty of Western Siberia- Elements of Shamanism as a Form of
        Cultural Identity."

SacredHoop.org. "Mirrors of the Soul."

Sanders, Dr. Fabian. "Tibetan Oracles and Himalayan Shamans."

SARASWATI, DR. SWAMI SHANKARDEV. "Purifying the Five Elements of Our Being - Yoga
        Journal.Pdf>." *Yoga Journal.*

Theinnervoyage.com. "Soul Retrieval."

warpaths2peacepipes.com. "Shaman."

Wiki, Rigpa. "Eight Classes of Gods and Demons."

Wikipedia. "Babaylan."

———. "Bardo."

———. "Central Tibetan Administration."

———. "Chukchi People."

———. "Common Era."

———. "Cultural Revolution."

———. "Dalai Lama."

———. "Dissociation Psychology."

———. "Dzogchen."

———. "Forbidden City.Pdf."

———. "Genghis Khan."

———. "Khalkha Mongols."

———. "Manchu Shamanism."

———. "Neoshamanism."

———. "Palace of Earthly Tranquility."

———. "Prayer Flag."

———. "Psychopomp."

———. "Regional Forms of Shamanism."

———. "Reincarnation."

———. "Samoyedic Peoples."

———. "Shamanism."

———. "Shamanism in the Qing Dynasty."

———. "Shamanistic Remnants in Hungarian Folklore."
———. "Skandha."
———. "Sunyata."
———. "Tantra."
———. "Tenzin Wangyal Rinpoche."
———. "Tibet."
———. "Tibetan Empire."
Woolger, Dr. Roger J. "Beyond Death- Transition and the Afterlife."

www.ingramcontent.com/pod-product-compliance
Lightning Source LLC
Chambersburg PA
CBHW060814090426
42737CB00002B/62